# Just Stop Having Problems, Stupid!

## The Anti-Self-Help Guide

By Dr. Matt,
Fake Doctor

Just Stop Having Problems Stupid!
The Anti-Self-Help Guide

Third Edition (2011)


Visit Dr. Matt online at
TheDrMatt.com


To ask Dr. Matt questions,
email askdrmatt@gmail.com


Cover photography by Alex Rubin.
Photo editing by Matt Kump.

*For me, the person who wrote most of this book*

# *Introduction*

Many people have come to me over the years, at least half of them willingly, and most not under sedation. And of that half, some of those people have serious problems, and of those people, many of them do not know that I haven't the faintest idea what I can do for them. None.

You see, I'm not a bona fide "doctor" in the strictest sense; that is, in the sense that a "university" has granted me a "doctorate." My doctorate is what I call the doctorate of life. It wasn't handed to me by a "dean of students" on a "platform," unless that dean of students was life, and the platform was also life in a slightly different metaphorical sense.

So what do I do for those people who come to me and say, "Dr. Matt, I've got serious problems"?

Well, I tell them the same thing I'm going to say to you: "Stop having problems, stupid!"

## THAT'S WHAT I SAID!

It sounds simple, doesn't it? Just simply stop having problems. Some people say, "But Dr. Matt, I've got chronic depression." That sure sounds like a serious problem. Until you stop having it. Think about it. If you stop having it, then it doesn't exist, and that means it's no longer serious.

One person said to me, "Dr. Matt, I suffer from panic attacks."

I said, "Did you try not having them?"

They admitted they had never tried to simply not have them. They were just there, as if they just showed up one day and were there to stay.

Once the panic attacks started, they accepted them as something they had. That's stupid!

Now, I know some of you out there like to make things complicated. You think it's just too simple to stop having problems. You paid good money for this book, and now you want to see me work for it, to put my doctorate degree[1] to good use.

Well, I've got just the thing for you, oh negative nanny. This book is plum full of amusing anecdotes, inspirational speeches, doctoral jargon, and loads of other stuff that will get you to stop having problems, guaranteed[2].

Ready to get started stopping? Okay, then.

---

[1] Dr. Matt, as stated, does not have a doctorate degree granted by a university or other doctorate program.
[2] This is not an actual guarantee.

# The First Lesson

Imagine you're on a boat. The boat is one of those older boats, like the Mayflower, but with a different name. And it's riding along on choppy seas, with the storm coming in from the southeast. Can you picture this? You're on this boat, and you're sitting amidst a bunch of barrels. What do the barrels say on the side? Gunpowder. Water is starting to come up over the side of the boat, and the captain says to you that we've got to move those barrels below decks, not to the lowest decks, but to the middle-lower decks—this is kind of an old version of a cruise ship—where the barrels will be dry.

Now imagine that you move all those barrels, but then, all of the sudden, the storm stops, and it turns out that the barrels were not in any danger of getting wet. There was no point at all in moving them. Have you pictured all that? Good. Because moving those barrels was exactly like this exercise. It had absolutely no point. I did that to illustrate this point: clever metaphors will not suddenly enlighten you. That's stupid. Not only that, but there's no such thing as the middle-lower decks on a boat like that. How can that apply to your life when it doesn't even exist? It's sort of like your problems. You think there's a place inside you, inside your "boat" if you will, where your problems can reside, as if they really go there. But this place is just imaginary, but you don't know it because you don't know boats.

See what I mean? Make believe stories can't help you. You can't stop your problems by pretending. You have to stop your problems by stopping them.

Still not convinced? Neither was Sally. At first...

# You Think You're Messed Up? Talk to Sally

Sally was a single mother with three children, all of them under ten. If that wasn't bad enough, each of those children was from a different father, and each of those fathers was in jail or had been in jail. She was seriously overweight and had diabetes. She had a steady job, but she was underpaid and passed over for promotion again and again.

Now, when I met Sally and heard all this, I wanted to give her a big slap across the face. But because I am a professional, I decided to try a different approach.

I said to her, "Sally, look at all these problems around you. You've got to stop having them! Stop it, right now! Bad!"

Sally looked hurt. You see, it wasn't really her that was hurt, it was her problems, who'd set up shop in her middle-lower decks. They didn't want to leave, and they didn't want Sally to know that they were just barrels that could be thrown overboard. Sally's problems wanted Sally to think that *they* were *her*. So they told her to be upset, and protect them.

And that's just what happened. Sally got mad at me, insisting that it wasn't easy to just stop having problems, that everything always happened to her, and it wasn't her fault. Now, there's a phrase I coined (and I can say I coined it because I don't read something if I think it will have ideas that I've already had) called "playing the victim." Sally felt she was a victim of

12

everything around her, so she was not responsible for her problems. Well, maybe she was not
responsible for the very first barrel placed in her
middle-lower decks, but she didn't throw that
one overboard, even when she gained the
strength to do so. Why? Because after a while it
looks like part of the ship. And taking that barrel
down left the door open for other barrels to be
brought down, and all the deckhands are just
bringing down barrels. Why not? The captain of
the ship is Sally's ego, and the captain says,
"Look, I have a place where barrels go, that's just
the way it is." The real captain of the ship should
be Sally, but Sally is delusional and thinks that
she's just a deckhand. So, she actually *helps* the
deckhands, helping them move barrel after barrel
after barrel, stacking all this volatile powder in
one spot on a rocky ship.

You see? The captain, Sally's ego, is concerned with protecting the barrels, and in doing
so, endangers the entire ship. It's not worth it,

Sally, I wanted to say, just throw the barrels overboard.

I could see that, with Sally, I would have to try a different approach. She had so many barrels of gunpowder that she had run out of space and had begun to glue them to the ship's hull. Now, if that isn't dangerous I don't know what is. They really *had* become part of the boat.

The problem was that she thought the problems were a part of her and they belonged there. So, I did something that I'm going to teach to you. I went down to Sally's middle-lower decks (the subconscious, as the lower decks would be the unconscious), and I changed the labels on the barrels to something she would throw overboard.

Now, even though I hate metaphors, just to keep you up to speed, in this scenario I would be the visiting Admiral, recently come aboard from the HMS Bestest, put into service in 1778 by the

14

Queen, God save her. In this scenario, I also resemble Russell Crowe.

## Russell Crowe saves the day

Below decks, strutting in my Admiral gear, I saw the problem: each of the barrels had been stamped when they had been brought on board with the label "HMS Sally." Everything that came on board Sally's ship was identified as belonging to the ship. Between that label and the big letters above it that said, "Gunpowder," it had the brand of gunpowder: diabetes, bad relationships, weight gain, job stagnation.

So, just to be clear, a barrel would say, "Gunpowder." Below that, in a slightly smaller font, it would say, for example, "Diabetes." Then, below that, stamped in red ink, slightly askew, it said, "HMS Sally." Again, I look like Russell Crowe.

15

Here's what I did: I washed off that red stamp, and I put the stamp on of another ship. Actually, what I did was more like this. I washed off all the red stamps, and then I summoned a deckhand with my Admiral's whistle, and told that deckhand to go fetch Sally, and to do it quickly if he wanted his rations that night.

When Sally came, I said, "Look, Sally, none of these barrels are stamped with what ship they belong to."

At first, Sally was dismissive. "Oh, well they must belong to this ship because that's where they are now."

I replied, "Well, they all came from somewhere. Think hard. Where did this barrel come from?" I pointed to the barrel that was branded: "Weight Gain."

After talking about it for a while, Sally mentioned that her grandmother, who was overweight herself, had always had food to give. Food was how her grandmother gave love.

"Okay, then," I said, and slapped a stamp on that barrel: "HMS Grandmother."

I turned to another barrel, the one that said "Job Stagnation."

"What about this one?" I said. After some brainstorming, Sally mentioned that her father had always said she wasn't smart, and she should take the first job she could with job security. The barrel really should have said, "Lack of deservability." Oh, and what do you know, it said that on the back! Anyway, we stamped that one, "HMS Father."

Pretty soon, we had all the barrels stamped that we could find, and none of them said "HMS Sally."

What did I do next? I sent Sally away, and summoned the ship's current captain, Sally's ego. I said, "Look! This ship is weighed down with cargo, and it doesn't even belong on this ship! Did you tell all those other ships that they could leave their cargo here?" And of course she had not.

We did the only sensible thing, which was to toss overboard any cargo that did not belong to the HMS Sally. And you see, folks, it was *all* those barrels, all the problems, that did not belong there. They were just taking up space.

Now, for anyone who would find it inappropriate to simply toss someone else's cargo overboard rather than returning it, I will once again state this is why metaphors are stupid. But I will say this: when you are at sea, it's a matter of survival, and you will do whatever you must for the safety of that ship. If you put the ship at risk, you put yourself at risk. And it certainly is stupid to carry gunpowder if you do not have to, gunpowder that isn't even yours! Toss it overboard, let those other ships track it down if they really want it. (Incidentally, if you are going to be transporting gunpowder, it's good to put some distance between barrels, in my opinion.)

Obviously, we weren't actually on a ship; we did the equivalent as an exercise in my apartment / office. But the result was the same. Sally saw that whenever there was problem, it had been put there by somebody else.

There was still a bigger problem. Sally kept allowing new barrels onto the ship. Why? Because she wasn't the captain of her own ship. I would like to say that she became the captain eventually, but even Admiral Russell Crowe is not God. As I write this, I would say that although Sally is not captain, she's realized that she's not like the other deckhands. And perhaps it would be helpful if I would tell her the metaphor of the boat, but I hate metaphors.

How does one become the captain of one's ship? I'll tell you.

# The Poop Deck

Now, I don't know what a poop deck is, and I'm sure I could look it up on Wikipedia if I wanted to, or you could put this book down and do the same. My guess would be that it has nothing to do with excrement. This is the other problem with metaphors used in self-help books. A comparison will often be made to a subject that the author has not lived. I've never lived on a ship. Neither have you. Needless to say, comparisons that authors with PhDs make should be taken with a grain of salt. That's why my doctorate is more valuable than a typical doctorate, because it's the doctorate of life.

Often I'll see people who are chronic readers of self-help books, but they're no closer to help.

Why? Because they're more interested in knowing than doing. They'll say, "Oh, *now* I have perfect insight into the collective unconscious which has affected my archetype fantasies."

And then I'll say, "Oh yeah? Well, can you read a financial statement yet?"

"No," they say.

To that, I have one word: "Stupid."

I'm not saying the people are stupid, I'm saying the focus is stupid. The most incapable people are the smartest people I know. Advanced Calculus may be a piece of cake for them, but taking care of an overdue bill baffles them. Somehow, they've gotten the idea that the world is in their head. Well, sure, from a Carlos Casteneda / quantum physics level, reality is perception. But some knowledge is practical, and some knowledge just takes up space. Not everything is worth knowing.

## NOT EVERYTHING IS WORTH KNOWING

Gasp! Say it isn't so, Dr. Matt!

Yes, it is so. Knowledge is power, but so is Uranium 235, and you don't see me carrying that around with me everywhere I go. The problem is that really smart people believe that all knowledge is power, and what they don't factor in is time. You see, all knowledge takes time to acquire. There is practically a limitless supply of knowledge available, especially in this day and age. Yet, for us mortals, there is a limited supply of time. The way I see it, stuffing a huge variety of knowledge in one's cranium brings about diminishing returns, because there's only so much time available to utilize that knowledge. And anyone who has attended public schools will tell you: there is some knowledge that you will simply not use, without question.

True, what you will use and what you will not use cannot be determined for certain. But, at the very least, knowledge must be prioritized. If each piece of knowledge is a potential power source, then it's power output should be rated, even if it's only a guess. Even through wild guessing, it would become apparent that some knowledge is more powerful than other knowledge.

Here's another thing to consider: your body consumes energy to constantly replenish everything that your brain needs in order to hold memory. Therefore, knowledge consumes power. Think over everything that we've stated:

- **There is a limited amount of knowledge I can gain in one lifetime.**
- **Each piece of knowledge consumes power.**
- **Some pieces of knowledge produce more power than others.**

23

- **If I don't use it, some pieces of knowledge may consume more power than they produce.**
- **By selectively choosing what knowledge I acquire, I will determine if my net power output is a) positive or b) negative.**

Now, obviously, this is a stupid metaphor because the type of power consumed is not exactly the type of power produced. And I'm not suggesting you sit down and estimate the kilowatt hours that a piece of knowledge would consume, because that's stupid. I'm sure that there's some really smart person who really, really wants to figure that out, and may even do it, and this is why they waste power. It's simply not worth knowing. I don't care if you tell yourself, "Oh, I'll just get on the Google and look up the energy requirements of the human brain, and divide that by the number of facts a person retains at the end of their lifetime. Or, maybe I'll need to multiply the energy requirements of the entire human body by the percentage of body mass that the brain carries." To this, I ask you, have you considered the fact that the energy requirements for a human being are variable over a lifetime, as indeed fact retention must be? My apologies, you say, I didn't factor in those variables. And then I might mention the fact that what you really want to do is get a random sampling of individuals over all ages and body types. And certainly, you would want to examine gender differences and environmental factors.

What is this ridiculous process called? Science. Scientific method is what was created when we had the answers already but couldn't prove them. Einstein's Theory of Relativity was not "proven" until it's effect could be observed. Science has done some great things for us, but in our every day lives, scientific method has a great spot, and that's the poop deck.

Like I said before, I don't know what the poop deck is, but we'll say that's it's the place for knowledge that's useful sometimes, and really not useful other times. In other words, the net power output is sometimes positive, sometimes negative. At this point, we're mixing metaphors, which is stupid, so let's put this all in a power station.

## The Power Plant

Instead of the poop deck, certain knowledge is like the nuclear material in the water tanks. Put the material too low, and the power output is insufficient for the demand of the grid. Put it too high, and the power output is wonderful, but you increase the risk of meltdown. In this scenario, meltdown would be chaos in one's life, and I would be playing the part of Brian Williams from NBC Nightly News, warning you about the possible meltdown.

Where was I going with this?

Anyway, let's just summarize this chapter to say: knowledge is power, but some knowledge is not worth knowing. And, even of the knowledge that is worth knowing, some of that knowledge must be carefully monitored. As for the rest, shit, just let it roll.

# Captain You

What I was really wanting to get to was about being the captain of your own ship. Then we got onto that power plant metaphor, and, to me, the power plant is a much more boring metaphor to spend your time on than the ship at sea. I mean, if I had to choose, I would be Admiral Russell Crowe over Brian Williams any day.

It's true, Brian Williams is arguably more attractive than Russell Crowe, but Russell has a more imposing presence. I would say that Russell's attractiveness comes from his intensity and talent.

Some of you may complain that I'm going to teach you how to be the captain, while I am already an admiral. That's just because this is my stupid metaphor, and for your stupid metaphor, you can be whomever the heck you want to be. Just don't be Russell Crowe, because that would piss me off.

## An important note

If some of you were saying to yourselves, "Oh no, well I should choose someone different from Russell Crowe for my metaphors," I want to point out that this is stupid. Why the heck should you care if you piss me off? This is why this is an important note. It's not important to not piss people off. People are going to be pissed off at you regardless of what you do. I say again: someone being pissed off at you is a matter of choice: *their* choice, not yours. I decided that I would be pissed off if other people chose Russell Crowe, but that's my problem, not yours. Be

Russell Crowe if you want to. But, seriously, that will really piss me off.

This leads me to another point: just because I have the wherewithal to understand that being pissed off is my problem, that doesn't mean it's not going to happen. Put in another way: knowledge is power, but knowledge is not necessarily transformative. To transform you must act. What would stop me from being pissed off at you is not you choosing someone different from Russell Crowe. What if you chose someone else that would piss me off? I would probably be slightly pissed off if you chose Brian Williams, but I didn't say that. The only way to not be pissed off at you is for me to make a different choice. And a conscious choice is most definitely an action.

Since I don't really like that power plant metaphor, let's put that power back on the ship and make it manpower. Yes, all the deckhands constitute a great amount of power when combined and led properly. But if they are not led, the power does nothing. It simply exists, and meanwhile those deckhands need to be fed as you're just sitting out at sea. Where is this ship going, they want to know? If you do not lead them, disagreements will arise between them. It might get so bad as to create mutiny. They are not mutinous because they are bad men. They are mutinous because stagnation and poor leadership create mutiny. They need a strong captain. And that strong captain must be you.

Your ego is not the best captain, because an ego that is captain is only concerned with staying in charge, and not about giving solid leadership to the crew.

Here's the beautiful part: this is only true when the ego is captain. In other words, when you give the ego another role on the ship, the ego will happily do its job and be helpful in every way. The only time when the ego wants to be captain is when you're not doing your job as the rightful captain. And why not? The ego will go where its needed. If you want to be a deckhand on your own ship, then the ego will happily take charge.

Now, for some of you who want to know exactly what the ego is, don't worry about it. You have an idea of what I'm talking about, and that's good enough. You have an idea of what it means to have a bruised ego, or when someone is ego-maniacal. Don't go get a book on Sigmund Freud, or type "ego" into Wikipedia. It may give you a lot more knowledge about what the ego is, but that doesn't mean that knowledge will do you any good. Seriously, it doesn't matter, and that brings me to another important point:

## You know more than you know you know

Not only do you not need to go out and get all the knowledge you possibly can, but what I see with people is that the chronic self-helpers are those who don't trust the knowledge they already have, and indeed, will claim that they do *not* have it. They search and they search and read and read and ask questions of everyone, and meanwhile, they already know plenty. You know that book, "Everything I Needed to Know I Learned in Kindergarten"? I've never read it, but the title is the right idea. You already have 99% of what you need, but you just don't trust it. I mean, look at all the crap I know, and I don't have any sort of psychology "degree" or typical "doctorate."

I was an avid reader as a child, and I would often read books that had plenty of vocabulary words I didn't understand. Sometimes there would be at least one word on a page that was unfamiliar. I quickly learned that it didn't matter; I still understood the story perfectly. Never was one word so important as to unhinge an entire storyline. Never. I mean, I didn't know what the word "clitoris" meant, yet I still got the

33

gist of the story. Yet, people will fixate on what they don't know, or what they can't do, with laser beam focus.

The other day I passed a man coming out of a public restroom who only had one leg. He wasn't coming out in a wheelchair, even though the restroom was very wheelchair accessible. He had left his wheelchair outside, and was instead hopping on that leg. For some reason this seemed like a perfectly logical adaptation, but I realized that I had never seen this before for someone who only had one leg.

Often times we will marvel at this type of adaptation for someone who has lost a limb or won a fight against cancer. Yet, each and every one of us are infinitely more capable than we think; it's just more obvious for those that overcome physical challenges.

Some people would see that man hopping on one leg, and still insist that they are incapable of getting themselves out of debt, or out of depression, or changing any of their other life circumstances. It's the trick of, "Oh sure, other people can put a stop to their problems, but they're different." Or "My situation is different." Well, of course it is, but by setting yourself up to be special, what you are really doing is absolving yourself of responsibility, when you *know* you could be changing your circumstance.

If you *really* want to be special, do what I do: picture yourself as Superman.

# Superman

So, you've decided that you aren't like other people. You're special. The whole world is against you. Even God is against you. Or, for this example, let's say the great and powerful Zod is against you. If you don't know who Zod is, again, don't bother renting Superman 2. I'm sure you can infer that Zod is an enemy that could give Superman some trouble.

Do you think Superman says, "Oh great, even Zod is against me, so what hope do I have?" Superman knows he is special; he knows that in some ways, he has an unfair burden of challenges. But Superman knows that he is capable of facing any challenge. He doesn't necessarily know he will *win*. He just knows that he must face those challenges if he is going to be Superman. Even when he knows Lex Luther has some kryptonite, do you think Superman decides to give up and avoids bars where Lex might hang out? No, I'm sure, if he had to, he would build some sort of Kryptonite radiation suit, or better yet, convince Jimmy Olsen to sneak in and get the Kryptonite out of there. Bet you didn't think of that last idea, did you? Some people are discouraged by the fact that they can't build a Kryptonite radiation suit, and because they look at that with laser focus, they don't realize that they can just send in Jimmy Olsen. Because, of course, Kryptonite will not affect young Jimmy.

This is another good point: obstacles that seem insurmountable can be ridiculously simple to overcome if you seek help. That doesn't mean self-help books. If Superman looked in the self-help section in that situation, no author would anticipate his need to get around a Kryptonite problem.

**Superman to Barnes and Noble employee:** "Excuse me, but which book might help a superhero overcome a substance which is radioactive only to him?"

**Barnes and Noble employee:** "I'm not sure, let me look that up on my nifty computer."

**Superman:** "Sure thing, I'll wait."

**Barnes and Noble employee:** "I have a book by Dr. Laura called 'How to Stop a Radioactive Marriage.'"

**Superman:** "I don't think that helps."

Barnes and Noble may have great employees, and Dr. Laura may have some great books out there (although I doubt it), but this isn't going to help Superman. He needs to talk to someone like me, or talk to other people that are his peers, as long as they aren't Zods. What he could do is go to the Fortress of Solitude and put one of those crystal pieces into one of those little slots and talk to the ghost of Marlon Brando, but as far as metaphors go, this is a little stupid.

## AM I SURROUNDED BY ZODS?

Like I said, if you seek help, make sure that it's not from a Zod. What I mean is that sometimes someone will say to you, "Hey, I'm from Krypton too, let's be friends." But what they *really* want to say is, "Kneel before Zod." Believe it or not, some people who seem like they want to listen and help you with your problems do *not* want those problems to go away for you. They like the fact that you have problems; it makes them feel better about their own captain-less ship, and they will give you advice which seems sound, but will, in fact, keep you in the same crappy place where you are at right now. Often, you will end up worse off than you were before. But they are clever enough so that you won't see that they contributed to this. In fact, they may seem to try even harder to help you. Be clear: not everyone who wants to help you is your friend. Some are Zods, and if they can't have world domination, they will do the next best thing: domination of you.

How do you know if someone is a Zod? Here are some telltale signs:

- *Zods will:* **use Krypton breath to blow over buses full of innocent people.**

  *Translation:* **they will unfairly judge others, even when it's in your favor.**

- *Zods will:* **offer to let you live, if you will serve only them.**

  *Translation:* **they will demand that you owe them for all the "help" they've given you.**

40

- *Zods will:* **throw large chunks of debris on top of you**

  *Translation:* **they will exhaust you with their endless complaining. Again, sometimes that complaining is about what's happening to *you*, so don't mistake this for sympathy. They are really just a Zod.**

Zods, in essence, take responsibility for nothing, yet feel they deserve everything. Beware of Zods, be on your guard around them at all times, and whatever you do, do not kneel before them.

## WHAT IS SUPERMAN, REALLY?

As I said before, if I want to be special, I picture myself as Superman. Superman, to me, represents the infinite potential of all mankind. A lot of people think that Superman does things

41

that no human could do because he is, in fact, an alien from Krypton. So let me get this straight: he has enough of a match of genetic material to look exactly like a human in every way, yet no human can do any of the things that he can? I choose to believe differently. Superman is like Jesus; he is a being who has discovered that he is capable of something greater.

Comics are a way of passing on history in a more digestible form, so a carpenter from Nazareth becomes a politician's son from Krypton. Jesus had a robe and beard as his "uniform," and Superman has a cape and that big "S". Other than that, pretty similar.

Anyway, we're all capable of something more. And before you make that something ethereal, look at your own life and what you've already decided is not possible. Is it really the case, or have you become your *own* Zod? Really, there are only two choices, be Superman, or be Zod. A lot of people want to be Jimmy Olsen, but even Jimmy is like an unrealized Superman. What if Superman was not the *first* to arrive from Krypton. What if he was the *last*, so therefore he hadn't yet lost the knowledge of his potential. Think about *that*.

# Time for another story

A man came into my apartment / office one day whom I will call "Director / Producer Steven Spielberg." Obviously, this is not his real name, and incidentally, Sally *was* that other woman's real name, so if you see her on the street, please don't mention the ship metaphor to her, because I haven't talked to her about that yet. Just to be sure you avoid the right person, her full name is Sally Ann Bopkins.

Anyway, this other man said to me, "You know, I made these three movies about the force and this galaxy far, far away, but I'm not sure what to do next."

These three movies, which I will not name for confidentiality reasons had done very well, yet they had become this man's entire identity. He was plagued by them. He was filled with fear about doing anything but that. He was, at the time, thinking about doing three more movies in the same universe.

So I said to him, "George, those movies did very well, but it's time to move on. Time is ever flowing onward, and we are always changing, making new choices. You can't make the same choice for yourself that you did 20 years ago. You are simply not in the same place. I mean, that's just stupid."

Needless to say, this man did not take my advice, and he went ahead and made another three movies, trying to recapture his past. I don't have to tell you what you already guessed: they were not nearly as good as his first three movies. In fact, they ranged from mediocre to crapioca (a mixture of crap and tapioca). There was even this part at the end when the main character has just been fitted with a mobile life support system, and learns that he is responsible for killing his wife, Padme. He screams "No!" in such an over-dramatic, ridiculous way that I literally fell out of my chair laughing. Had I not been laughing, I would have been crying at the travesty before me. I wish I could tell you the name of the movie, but trust me, it's not worth knowing. That's not to say that this "Steven Spielberg" is a bad filmmaker; he just got trapped in what many of us get trapped in: letting fear keep us from moving forward.

## THE FEAR TRAP

Let's go back to the ship. You're out in the ocean. You've got all these deckhands who are willing to be led. They will accept you as captain if you will only do so. What's preventing you? Fear. Fear is preventing you from becoming the captain, because you are afraid of what will come of it. You will have to pick a direction to sail, and ultimately, you will be responsible for it.

It's time to ask yourself: what are you afraid of? Picking the wrong destination? Well, let's just point out something. When you're sitting in the middle of the ocean, *any* destination is better than being indecisive. Well, no, you say, some destinations could place me in a precarious position, like meeting cannibals on an island. So what? It's either sail at the *risk* of being eaten by cannibals, or do nothing and be assured of death. Most people seriously do not consider that doing nothing is a riskier behavior than any of the choices they consider "risky."

I mean, look, if you were to be eaten by cannibals, at least you gave someone a good meal. If you die at sea, you're nibbled apart by fish or, at best, sharks and, at worst, rats on the ship.

Generally, fear is as stupid as the previous metaphor. In today's day and age, we will very rarely feel fear at the only time when we need it:

when our lives are in danger. You're not really at
sea, and you're not in danger of sailing into cannibals. So what are you so afraid of? Even if
death *is* a possible risk, can you absolutely,
assuredly *prevent* your death by doing something
different?

When someone dies in a mountain climbing
accident, a news reporter will talk about the fact
that mountain climbing is risky. Why? Because
they died? Did we not expect that person to die
at some point?

You see, "risk" is only defined by the likeli-
hood of what someone considers a "bad" outcome. Death is apparently considered the worst
of outcomes, but think about this: we, as individuals, are the single greatest contributor to our
own death, yet no one advocates putting warning
labels on our foreheads that state: "SURGEON
GENERAL'S WARNING: ALLOWING THIS
PERSON TO LIVE AS THEY SEE FIT HAS
BEEN SHOWN TO BE A CAUSE OF DEATH."

You must live your life, you must make the decisions that you must, regardless of risk, regardless of who gets pissed off at you, and regardless of what Zods say to you. As I said before, action, not simply knowledge, is what moves the ship. It's what leads the ship to treasures, and nothing else. If the deckhands spend all their time reading books about treasure finding, sailing techniques, and proper deck swabbing, then they will be the most knowledgeable drowning victims alive.

# But I still have problems!

Ah yes, the problems. The barrels and barrels of problems. Do you know what? A ship will still sail beautifully, even with some barrels on the middle-lower decks. A ship will still sail, even if fear is preventing you from being the captain. Didn't I tell you that your ego was ready to take over, if you aren't?

The problem isn't your problems. The problem is that you think your problems are so damn important. Stop it. Right now.

You think that your problems are so large that they prevent you from sailing. They don't. They aren't. You are saying to yourself that I

50

don't know *your* problems, and boy, are they massive. Question: are you currently naked in a large pot with steaming hot water, and natives are chopping carrots into the pot? Or: have you been mountain climbing, and a two-ton boulder has just shifted and pinned your arm against the rock face?

If the answer to both of these questions is no, then your problems are not as important or as insurmountable as you think they are. They simply aren't. No. NO. Don't make that face at me.

But, you say, why on earth would they *seem* so large and overwhelming if they are not?

Because some idiot labeled the barrels "Gunpowder," when they are in fact filled with nothing but dry dirt. That's right, those barrels that your captain made you move oh so carefully, that were labeled oh so carefully, and you even were smart enough to space apart so that a potential explosion would not destroy absolutely everything... dirt. Nutrition-less dirt that would not even grow plants. Trust me, I'm as surprised as you are. Someone wanted you to believe that the barrels were both important and that they were yours. Who was it? Does it matter? Who-ever it was, he/she is an asshole. Because I've been carrying around friggin' dirt, and even lamenting the fact that I threw some of it over-board.

Are you ready to throw those overboard yet? Why are you still carrying those problems? If you're still not ready, then it would make sense to ask yourself why it's so important to have dirt in your cargo. For some people, it *is* important. For Zod's, they can tell everyone about how people put dirt in their cargo, and say wonder-fully nasty things about HMS Father for the rest of their life. Never mind the fact that they could have thrown it all overboard. For others, they can keep putting barrels onto their ship until it *is* in danger of sinking, and then call for aid so people can see how helpless their ship is.

You want to know what happened to us? We made it, as a civilization. We grew and we grew and we reached a point where any of us can achieve practically anything. We saw the great, unexplored ocean in front of us, and we got scared. We were no longer encumbered by famine, plague, short life spans, or lack of freedom. So we had to make a reason for our fear, an excuse for why were not sailing off into our destinies. So we hired someone to take some barrels, fill them with dirt, and label them "Gunpowder," and then put labels like depression, anxiety, and debt underneath them. We told them to put them on as many ships as they could. Then, we forgot all about the incident. You want to know who the asshole was? You and me, buddy.

## Get started stopping

The great thing about this is that the only one standing in your way is you. You are Superman. You are Brian Williams. It's possible that you are even Russell Crowe (but don't push your luck). You want to stop having problems? Just stop having them. Stop thinking about them 24/7. Stop telling people you have them. Tell people you have the opposite. Tell yourself you have the opposite. I've heard of people who stopped having cancer because they denied that they had it. Haven't you heard the phrase: "Never underestimate the power of denial?" Usually, this is meant as a negative statement. But it works both ways.

You're thinking to yourself, "But I have depression." No, you don't. "But my doctor diagnosed me." Well, I'm a doctor and I say otherwise[3]. "But depression is caused by a chemical

---

[3] Dr. Matt is not a real doctor. His advice is for the purpose of entertainment only and should not be

imbalance or some other science-generated excuse for what I've already decided is true." Okay, you have depression, that's your choice. That's right, your choice. But don't mistake it for anything but choice.

You still don't believe me, do you? That you can just decide to not have problems? Why, have you tried it? If you still have trouble believing this, then I guess you believe in scientific method. Very well then, we'll try it your way.

Here is the hypothesis: you can stop having problems just by deciding. Now, go out and test this hypothesis. And it must be tested on you because this is about your problems. We want a good amount of data, so you should test this over a year. During that time, decide you do not have the problems you think you do. And remember, *deciding* is a matter of *action*. So you must *act* as one who does not have the problem you think you do. In your case, sir, you believe you are

---

considered medically sound.

incapable of being outgoing and social. Well, we are testing your ability to decide otherwise, so henceforth, you are outgoing and social. Now that we have decided, you will do the things that outgoing, social people do. You will spontaneously call friends. You will randomly talk to people in bars. You will flirt without caring what the outcome would be.

Obviously, if you are Jimmy Olsen trying to be Superman, I would not suggest that you prove your ability to be Superman by trying to leap buildings. Instead, start hitting on Lois Lane.

If you are overweight, madam, from now on you are thin. When you see yourself, deny there is any fat showing. Do what thin people do. Thin people go on walks, thin people dress in sexy clothes, thin people eat salad like it's the best food ever invented. Seriously, have you ever seen thin people just take handfuls of lettuce and eat it the way I eat Hint-of-Lime Tostitos™? I've seen it, and it looks bizarre, but it's what thin people do.

Wait a minute, you say to me, I see what you're doing. If people do those things, they will become what they say they already are. Oh, so you want to withdraw your challenge to my hypothesis that you can stop having problems by deciding to stop having them? You thought it was stupid. Now it seems not so stupid?

## WHAT'S REALLY STUPID

I'll tell you what's stupid: hanging on to problems. They're not yours, and they're not you. You don't "have" them, you don't even own them. They were put on your ship, so throw them out and then get the hell on your way. If for nothing else, do it because I am Admiral Russell Crowe, and I've given you a direct order.

# Coming to the End

Are we at the end already, you say? Yes, don't you have enough information to get started stopping? Let me put it this way: if I'm Superman, carrying a ship full of Uranium 235 to a power plant, I can't concern myself with extraneous details. I've given you what you need, the most compact pieces of knowledge that will yield the greatest returns. Any more than this and the power conversion ratio will not be as great.

Put another way: adding 20 more sails to the ship is not necessarily going to make it faster, and adding 20 more chapters to this book will not necessarily make it more effective. You got the basics, but let's help you out by giving you the cliff notes. In fact, you can read just read this chapter if you want to, and I apologize for not mentioning that sooner.

## CLIFF NOTES

- You can stop having problems by deciding to stop having them.
- Clever metaphors will not suddenly enlighten you. (Also: I hate metaphors.)
- Not every barrel on your ship is cargo that belongs there, no matter how it was stamped.
- Your ego does not belong as captain, and would be better suited to another position.
- Your problems are not really yours. They were mislabeled as yours when they were brought on board. Throw them overboard.
- I don't know what a poop deck is.

- Not all knowledge is worth knowing.
- Russell Crowe is more attractive than Brian Williams.
- Be willing to piss people off. (Except Russell Crowe.)
- You know more than you know you know.
- Even Superman might encounter situations where he would need to ask for help from Jimmy Olsen.
- Do not, under any circumstances, kneel before Zod.
- Fear is largely useless. Chances are, you're going to die no matter what you do.
- Your problems are not as important as you think they are.
- A decision must be an action. Want to stop having problems? Act like it.

# That's it.

*Now, stop having problems, stupid!*

# About the Author

Dr. Matt has repeatedly distinguished himself in the fake profession community and the establishment of Doctors Who Aren't Doctors™.

I don't mean to say he's distinguished himself with repeated accomplishments. I mean to say that he's distinguished himself repeatedly every time someone buys this book. So, if you're worried about his credentials, purchase the book first, and that will automatically add validation to his credentials, which in turn, garners trust. If you're still not sure, buy another book, and just keep buying until the feeling goes away. They make great gifts, and they're perfect for setting in a book stand in the bathroom. Two trips to the bathroom and you can have this book finished. That's how incredibly efficient it is.[4]

Dr. Matt lives in Vancouver, B.C.

---

[4] Actual bathroom time will vary.

# THE NEXT BOOK BY DR. MATT

## When It Comes To Relationships, You've Been An Idiot

*Find it now on Amazon.com!*